St. John's School

Given by
Leon & Linda Stepanian

In honor of
Reese Stepanian

Book Fair 2011

ANIMALS UNDERGROUND
BADGERS

EMILY SEBASTIAN

PowerKiDS press™

New York

Published in 2012 by The Rosen Publishing Group, Inc.
29 East 21st Street, New York, NY 10010

First Edition

Editor: Amelie von Zumbusch
Book Design: Julio Gil

Photo Credits: Cover, back cover (badger) Norbert Rosing/National Geographic/Getty Images; back cover (armadillo, fox, mongoose), pp. 10–11, 24 (bottom left) Shutterstock.com; back cover (chipmunk) James Hager/Robert Harding World Imagery/Getty Images; back cover (mole) Geoff du Feu/Stone/Getty Images; pp. 5, 24 (bottom right) David W. Hamilton/Riser/Getty Images; pp. 6–7, 24 (top right) Steve & Ann Toon/Robert Harding World Imagery/Getty Images; pp. 9, 24 (top left) Comstock/Thinkstock; p. 13 Jupiterimages/Photos.com/Thinkstock; p. 15 iStockphoto/Thinkstock; p. 17 Robin Redfern/Photolibrary/Getty Images; pp. 18–19 Mr. Elliott Neep/Photolibrary/Getty Images; p. 21 Joe McDonald/Visuals Unlimited/Getty Images; p. 23 Thomas Kokta/Workbook Stock/Getty Images.

Library of Congress Cataloging-in-Publication Data

Sebastian, Emily.
  Badgers / by Emily Sebastian. — 1st ed.
      p. cm. — (Animals underground)
  Includes index.
  ISBN 978-1-4488-4955-0 (library binding) — ISBN 978-1-4488-5060-0 (pbk.) —
ISBN 978-1-4488-5061-7 (6-pack)
  1. Badgers—Juvenile literature. I. Title.
  QL737.C25S43 2012
  599.76'7—dc22
                                        2010050966

Manufactured in the United States of America

CPSIA Compliance Information: Batch #WS11PK: For Further Information contact Rosen Publishing, New York, New York at 1-800-237-9932

CONTENTS

Badgers are smart and strong.
They are known for their **stripes**.

Baby badgers are called **cubs**. Males are boars, while females are sows.

American badgers live on North America's Great Plains. These are big grasslands.

Eurasian badgers live in Europe and Asia. They are bigger than American badgers.

American badgers most often live alone. Eurasian badgers live in groups, called clans.

Badgers are great diggers. The dens they dig are often known as setts.

Eurasian badger setts have many tunnels. Some clans live in setts dug by their grandparents.

Eurasian badgers are good hunters. They eat mostly bugs, worms, and fruit.

American badgers eat small animals. They dig these animals out of the ground.

Badgers are fighters. They will charge at bears, wolves, and mountain lions.

Words to Know

American badger

cub

Eurasian badger

stripe

Index

Web Sites

Due to the changing nature of Internet links, PowerKids Press has developed an online list of Web sites related to the subject of this book. This site is updated regularly. Please use this link to access the list:

www.powerkidslinks.com/anun/badgers/